MW01602328

Grief Demystified

GRIEF DEMYSTIFIED

A COMPANION THROUGH CHANGE

BRENDA J. DeMOTTE

ISBNs: 978-0-9975465-3-8 (paperback); 978-0-9975465-4-5 (ePub); 978-0-9975465-5-2 (Kindle)

Printed in the United States of America
First Printing: 2016

20 19 18 17 16   5 4 3 2 1

Cover and interior design by Ryan Scheife / Mayfly Design

To order, visit Griefdemystified.com

Contents

INTRODUCTION

Because your experience of grief is and will be unique, this notebook provides brief summaries of each chapter from my book, *Grief Demystified,* with lots of room for your notes. The unlined white space invites you to jot down thoughts, to draw or paste photos, or maybe to create a mixture of words and images. Page pockets are there if you want to save mementos or clip articles that speak to you and your loss.

If you don't ordinarily keep a journal or sketchbook, think of this as a temporary doodle pad or scrapbook to use as you get through the seasons of your grief. Journal, memory book, reference book—use these pages however you wish. It's your own rough account or sketchy report. Tear out the blank pages for grocery lists if you have no other use for them.

Will writing, drawing, or pasting in photos about your loss make you sadder about it? That depends. Generally, if you use the blank space to express strong emotion, you will experience release. You feel something, and you get it out by expressing it. However, making yourself write when you feel blank, numb, or passive may not be helpful at all. There's no sense in drumming up negative feelings. The point is to discover whatever you do feel, and to do it your way.

If you are not usually introspective, you may wonder where to start. The writing prompts are there to help you or to ignore. Do it your way.

CHANGE ARRIVES WITHOUT WARNING

(Chapter One, *Grief Demystified*)

The crux of the matter:

When change is unexpected and unwelcome, you find that you can't cope normally. Your life has veered from the plans you had. No formula exists for weathering grief. Yet loss has always been a part of life. Help may come from our elders, from the wisdom of those who have gone before.

How would you describe the change in your life?

List a couple of ways that your loss has affected other parts of your life.

What's your hunch about sources of wisdom to help you through? People who might know more?

Other thoughts?

THE DUAL NATURE OF CHANGE

(Chapter Two, *Grief Demystified*)

The crux of the matter:

Every life change brings both loss and gain, both happiness and sadness. Even when a major life loss seems nothing but pointless and sad, unexpected benefits often appear. What you learn from hard experience may help you in ways that you can't imagine, especially at first.

What are you noticing about your grief? How might you use what you've noticed?

Jot down a couple of unexpected things that have come out of your loss.

Can you bring yourself to appreciate and even enjoy those things?

Other thoughts?

GRIEF REDEFINED

(Chapter Three, *Grief Demystified*)

The crux of the matter:

Grief brings strong emotions. You expect sadness and shock and maybe some anger. But you may be surprised to feel confused or enraged. You may feel irrationally guilty. You may experience the loss as a blow to your self-esteem and, at the same time, feel pressure to look and sound right. Could grief simply be the loss of an old self and the eventual discovery and definition of a new self?

What emotions have you noted so far?

Are there other emotions, not listed above, that you notice in yourself?

If your old self seems gone, how have you noticed that? Any thoughts or hopes about who your new self might be?

Other thoughts?

The Mechanics of Grief

DENIAL

(Chapter Four, *Grief Demystified*)

The crux of the matter:

It's natural to respond to major loss by saying, "I can't believe it," or feeling that the news just won't sink in. We can call this denial. But it may be more a postponement than a willful evasion of facts. The numb feeling or the I-can't-believe feeling is often a physical response in the body that cushions you from the harshness of loss.

Have you heard yourself or someone else say, "I can't believe it," about your loss?

Any thoughts about that?

What do you know about trauma from past experience?

Other thoughts?

ANGER

(Chapter Five, *Grief Demystified*)

The crux of the matter:

When the numbness of early grief wanes, you may find yourself irritable or angry. This may be why bereaved families tend to fight. Anger is energetic and can be helpful in clarifying matters. For instance, your anger may help you see what you fear. You may want to exercise caution when angry, however, to avoid saying or doing something you later regret.

Do you notice anger or irritability in yourself? Or in others who may be mourning the loss with you? How are you expressing it?

Is there any way anger might be helping you? Any thoughts about caution when angry? Do you find a link to any fears?

Other thoughts?

PHYSICAL SYMPTOMS
(Chapter Six, *Grief Demystified*)

The crux of the matter:

Physical symptoms often come with grief and loss. Digestive problems, difficulty breathing, loss of appetite, and difficulty sleeping are common. You may find extra rest and sleep, nutritious meals, and vigorous exercise especially helpful right now.

This could be a time to take care of yourself better than you ever have before.

How is your physical self today? Is there anything your body might be asking for?

What are you already doing that seems to help physically? Is there some way you could take even better care of yourself?

Other thoughts?

Partners and Grief

(Chapter Seven, *Grief Demystified*)

The crux of the matter:

We rarely grieve alone, but everyone grieves differently. Your best friend, spouse, sibling, or close colleague may approach the loss in a way that alarms you or makes you angry. Relaxing expectations can help. Can you find a way to lay aside expectations and bring curiosity to how your loved ones handle grief?

Have you noticed anything that surprised you in the way someone close to you is grieving or responding to your grief?

What do you expect of yourself and others?

Other thoughts?

RESTLESSNESS

(Chapter Eight, *Grief Demystified*)

The crux of the matter:

As the reality of your loss sinks in, you may get the jitters. Many of us, while grieving, become restless to the point that sleep is disrupted. It rarely works to keep still when you're jittery. You probably need to move. Exercise improves sleep and appetite. Anything you can think of to move with the restlessness may help.

Have you noticed any restlessness? What thoughts and feelings go along with that? How's your sleep?

What about exercise? What do you think: are you getting enough? Is there anything you'd like to alter about the way or how much you exercise?

Other thoughts?

DISORGANIZATION

(Chapter Nine, *Grief Demystified*)

The crux of the matter:

As unexpected as it may be, a disorganized feeling is common in grief. There are decisions to make and others may pressure you to do so. Yet you find your thoughts foggy and unfocused. You may even think something is wrong with your brain. But grief is strenuous inner work. Disorganization may just be a sign of how hard you are working.

Do you notice any difficulty in focusing on practical matters or making decisions? How have you been coping? Is there any way to take the pressure off?

What inner search might be absorbing your energy?

Other thoughts?

PREOCCUPATION

(Chapter Ten, *Grief Demystified*)

The crux of the chapter:

Grief often brings preoccupation with troubling thoughts. Doubts or guilt feelings may plague you, as well as fears about what others think of you. Your doubts may put you at odds with your faith community or social group. These nagging thoughts, though painful, signal a need to make order out of the chaos. One day soon you may be ready for that.

Have you noticed any unwanted thoughts or feelings? Any doubts that don't seem to go away?

How do you feel you are fitting into your faith community or social group? Anything about that you want to explore here?

Other thoughts?

Searching

(Chapter Eleven, *Grief Demystified*)

The crux of the matter:

The experience of loss challenges the most basic beliefs about what life means. In bereavement, you naturally question whatever you thought was true before the loss. You search for new truth that makes sense of things, including the loss. The search can make you feel set apart and at odds with family, friends, and social circles. But redefining your beliefs is an essential part of redefining yourself.

Have you noticed yourself questioning what you previously thought was true? What beliefs pop to mind for re-evaluation?

What's the new truth for you today? Where have you recently found peace?

Other thoughts?

RESIGNATION

(Chapter Twelve, *Grief Demystified*)

The crux of the matter:

Grief often brings moments of resignation. You see that there's no way out of the loss. It's brutal and it's forever. But as the new truths you're learning get clearer, your honesty gets stronger and stronger. These are the cards that you've been dealt. You hate this hand, but you know you've got to play it.

Have you noticed any no-way-out moments? Any new truths?

What are the cards in the hand you've been dealt?

Other thoughts?

ISOLATION

(Chapter Thirteen, *Grief Demystified*)

The crux of the matter:

Your loss may seem to set you apart while the rest of the world goes on. Spending time alone while grieving is natural. If you desire solitude, you may need to take charge and get some time alone, regardless of what anyone else thinks. You will likely find yourself able to reconnect with friends and family when the time is right.

What do you need today in the way of human contact?

What happens when you are alone with your grief? How are your thoughts and feelings different?

Is there a point in your solitude when you feel you've had enough alone time? How do you know?

How could solitude be your friend?

Other thoughts?

REORGANIZATION

(Chapter Fourteen, *Grief Demystified*)

The crux of the matter:

At a time of loss, practical matters often demand your attention. You may need to reorganize your whole life, even when your energy is spent. You're likely to move forward, because you have to. But reorganization may befriend you in your grief. The decisions you make will likely express who you are becoming after the loss.

Have you found yourself changing something? What's the change? What does it mean to you?

Do you see any changes in your big picture? What do you see?

Other thoughts?

The Human Response to Change

Myths About Grief
(Chapter Fifteen, *Grief Demystified*)

The crux of the matter:

Myths about grief that are untrue can make loss more difficult to bear. For example, despite books, articles, and common sayings, grief rarely leads you through orderly stages. Grief almost never follows a recognizable path or moves in a smooth progression. And grief rarely ends completely.

What did you used to think about grief that doesn't seem true now? What are you noticing about your grief that you never expected?

What would you say to someone newly bereaved based on what you know now?

Other thoughts?

Before Taking Action

(Chapter Sixteen, *Grief Demystified*)

The crux of the matter:

Grief is chaotic. Before you take action, you may benefit from noticing your physical state and your mood. Grief often brings periods of anxiety. Finding ways to work with anxiety can help clarify what to do next. Likewise, working with feeling empty or despondent may help before you take action.

What have you noticed lately about your physical state? Any thoughts about how your physical state influences your actions?

What have you noticed lately about your moods? Where are those moods taking you?

Other thoughts?

TOOLS FOR WORKING WITH GRIEF

(Chapter Seventeen, *Grief Demystified*)

The crux of the matter:

While you are grieving, attempts to control your environment or other people usually fail. However, grief tools—simple, specific actions—can help you manage. For example, turning judgments into questions is a simple cognitive tool. As you translate your own harsh judgments into questions, you may feel relief from having to know. Writing out your thoughts and feelings can bring release. You can go for a walk to pace yourself with your grief. Your own ideas may be the best source of simple actions that might work for you.

Have you noticed inner judgments you may be making about yourself and other people? What, for instance? If you were to turn the judgment into a question, what would the question be?

What has helped you find release as you grieve? Would a walk help? What might help just as much?

Other thoughts?

SKILLS FOR LETTING GO
(Chapter Eighteen, *Grief Demystified*)

The crux of the matter:

It takes skill to slow down enough to allow yourself to grieve. Letting go may appear to be aimless or lazy, but because grief requires you to redefine yourself internally, you may need to conserve energy. There are lots of ways to let go. Allowing yourself to wallow in sadness may be useful at times. You can avoid people who are likely to upset you, and seek those with whom you feel safe. You can take breaks from grief by seeking distraction. Your own ideas of how to let go may be the best source of all.

Have you noticed yourself letting go lately? How did you do that? How did you feel about it?

What about avoiding people whom you find upsetting as you grieve? How can you manage to do that?

What are your hunches about other ways to let go? Do you dare wallow? What happens when you do? What about distractions?

Other thoughts?

SKILLS FOR GETTING YOURSELF GOING
(Chapter Nineteen, *Grief Demystified*)

The crux of the matter:

To keep from becoming overwhelmed by your loss, you may need to stir your energy. Daily tasks can help you stay in the here-and-now. Exercise or sports that require focus can be energizing. Playing a musical instrument can work the same way, or any hobby that requires focus. Actively connecting with people you want to see can help you cope. Helping others can be especially balancing.

Have you noticed difficulty staying in the here-and-now? Thoughts about that?

What seems to help you feel more energy? How are daily tasks affecting you? Exercise? Is there anything you'd like to alter about keeping your energy going?

Other thoughts?

DIFFERENT ORIENTATIONS TO GRIEF

(Chapter Twenty, *Grief Demystified*)

The crux of the matter:

People experience and approach grief differently. Some outwardly show emotion. Others express their grief through actions to honor what or who was lost. Some move through grief more quickly than others. Some delay the feelings and the actions that acknowledge their grief.

What have you noticed about your way of grief? Do you express emotion openly? Do you find action a more natural approach?

What about your pace of grieving? How would you describe it?

Any other thoughts about the way you grieve?

Men, Women, and Children in Grief
(Chapter Twenty-One, *Grief Demystified*)

The crux of the matter:

Men and women sometimes differ greatly in the way they grieve. Children have a separate set of challenges in how they understand and express their loss. These differences can bewilder us and cause conflict. Awareness and acceptance of how and why we differ can help us support one another.

Do you notice any gender role influence in how you grieve? In how others around you grieve? Thoughts about that?

What do you remember of your experience of grief as a child? If children share your current loss, how would you describe their way of grieving?

Do you notice any conflicts between the way you grieve and someone else's way? Thoughts about that?

Other thoughts?

The Facts of Loss

(Chapter Twenty-Two, *Grief Demystified*)

The crux of the matter:

We move through the shock of loss partly by facing the facts. Facing the physical details—exactly how the loss happened—we begin to comprehend and to grieve. Rituals such as funerals and memorial services give us a public way to face the facts, witnessed by family and friends.

What are the facts of your loss? Try writing them down or drawing them.

What thoughts come from what you write or draw?

How are you commemorating your loss? Is there a public aspect? Is there a private, personal aspect?

Other thoughts?

THE ARTIFACTS OF LOSS

(Chapter Twenty-Three, *Grief Demystified*)

The crux of the matter:

Belongings associated with what or whom was lost tend to hold ritual power for mourners. Touching and using these objects can help you face and release grief.

What physical objects associated with your loss come to mind? You might list each object and the meaning it has for you.

Do any of these objects or belongings have a practical use? Can you put such an object into use again? What thoughts and feelings arise when you do?

Other thoughts?

STORIES AS ARTIFACTS OF LOSS

(Chapter Twenty-Three, *Grief Demystified*)

The crux of the matter:

Telling a story about what or whom you have lost is an ancient and useful way to grieve. Places and things come to life again and real people show up in a story. A good story is cathartic and brings release. You can find freedom, sadness, and even humor there.

What stories associated with your loss come to mind? You might jot down a story or two and the meaning it has for you.

Do you dare remember a story about what or whom you lost that has a goofy or embarrassing or negative aspect? What thoughts and feelings arise when you do?

Other thoughts?

Touchstones for Grief Work
(Chapter Twenty-Five, *Grief Demystified*)

The crux of the matter:

Personal touchstones, such as objects, special words, or even particular people can release grief. Contact with these touchstones can help.

What would you say are the personal touchstones connected with your loss?

Are there words—a prayer, a song, or a book—that bring a sense of what or whom you lost? Jot down anything that comes to mind here. Perhaps sing or hum the song if you've got one.

A person can serve as a touchstone. Is there anyone you know who feels safer than others? Someone with whom you can share your grief? Can you seek more time with that person?

Other thoughts?

THE GEOGRAPHY OF GRIEF

(Chapter Twenty-Six, *Grief Demystified*)

The crux of the matter:

The places you associate with your loss can serve as potent reminders that open you to your grief. Likewise, public places where people openly grieve, such as monuments, places of worship, and especially cemeteries can be useful to visit.

What place or places do you associate with your loss?

Do you feel drawn to monuments, graves, or cemeteries as places to grieve? What other places call to you now? Can you make plans to go to such a place?

How would you converse with what or whom you lost? Is there a natural place where you could do that?

Other thoughts?

Faith and Doubt

(Chapter Twenty-Seven, *Grief Demystified*)

The crux of the matter:

Loss tends to throw into question every certainty about life. You may find that you need to remake your beliefs in the light of your new, hard experience. This task, though uncomfortable for many, can bring a new sense of balance about life.

What did you believe about life before your loss? Has anything changed about your beliefs since your loss?

What happens inside you when you let yourself doubt what you once believed? Can you allow yourself to doubt as a way to redefine your beliefs?

As you give yourself permission to redefine your beliefs, what do you believe now?

Other thoughts?

GRIEF AND MEMORY

(Chapter Twenty-Eight, *Grief Demystified*)

The crux of the matter:

Meaning often lies hidden in memories. When we allow ourselves to suffer memory's sting, we engage more deeply with grief. We can even come to a sense of wonder about what or whom we lost.

What memories associated with your loss come to mind? Jot a few down here.

What feelings and meaning do you associate with each memory?

If you allowed yourself to remember a bit more, what would come to mind?

Can you let yourself remember something dumb or ridiculous associated with your loss? What feelings arise if you do?

Other thoughts?

WHAT YOU GAIN FROM GRIEF AND LOSS

(Chapter Twenty-Nine, *Grief Demystified*)

The crux of the matter:

Loss tends to strip away the nonessentials and the illusions, leaving behind only those things that matter. You will likely notice small practical gains as you learn to live with your loss. Eventually, the sense of a new normal and a redefined self can bring major gains in maturity and resilience.

What used to matter before your loss that no longer seems so important now? Jot down a few ideas about that.

What practical gains have you already noticed? A new skill, such as handling what you previously had someone else handle for you? A new friend or a renewed friendship?

Do you have any sense of a new self? What might you like that new self to be? Any sense of what a new normal might look like for you? What it might feel like?

Other thoughts?

A Year Out? Ten Years Out? Closure?

(Chapter Thirty, *Grief Demystified*)

The crux of the matter:

Grief has no time limit and no tidy closure. You may not feel much better a year after your loss. A sight, sound, or a date on the calendar may trigger a fresh wave of grief. Even so, with careful thought, a new self and a more balanced view of life often emerge.

How long has it been since your loss? How does your grief seem now, compared to the beginning?

What seems to trigger a fresh wave of grief? Can you anticipate such triggers? Should you avoid them? Should you embrace them? What's the new meaning to be found?

Other thoughts?

About the Author

 Brenda grew up in a small farming community in southwestern, North Dakota. As a teenager she began working at the local funeral home. This work was the inspiration for her to become a funeral director, and ultimately, a psychotherapist specializing in grief and the psychology of change. This deep and rich resource of experience fostered the inspiration for this book *Grief Demystified*. Today, she is a professional speaker and educator on grief. Brenda resides in Apple Valley, MN with her husband, Jim.

Notes

Notes

Notes

Notes

Notes